Kid's Travel Journal – Disney Edition

Written by:

_____

(write your name here)

Cover and page design by Jeff Sechler - Copyright 2015

ISBN: 1508804656
ISBN-13: 978-1508804659

Printed in the U.S.A
2015 – First Edition

CONTENTS

How to use this book   1

Note to parents   2

Tips for getting ready   3

Preparing for my trip   4

My Disney Vacation!   10

Epcot World Showcase Passport   45

Disney Scavenger Hunts   57

     Magic Kingdom   58
     Epcot   59
     Animal Kingdom   60
     Hollywood Studios   61

Autographs   63

Games and Activities   105

More fun books by the author:

KID'S TRAVEL JOURNAL

Remember your trips forever in this easy to use travel journal
designed specifically for kids!
ISBN: 978-1490366913

ARE WE THERE YET?

Over 140 games, riddles and tongue twisters for hours of
traveling fun!
ISBN: 978-1463785444

BEGINNER WORD AND
NUMBER PUZZLES FOR KIDS

Word Search, Number Search and Crossword Puzzles for kids!
ISBN: 978-1475261622

MORE BEGINNER WORD AND
NUMBER PUZZLES FOR KIDS

Even more Word Search, Number Search and Crossword
Puzzles for kids!
ISBN: 978-1482384574

HOW TO USE THIS BOOK

To start, write your name on the cover using a permanent marker so that everyone knows it is yours!

Then, use this book to help make your visit to Disney even more fun. Write about your adventures and things that you did while traveling and visiting the most magical place on Earth. Make a list of items you will need to take with you and of all the exciting places you want to visit. Did you do something you might want to do again? Write it down! Did you eat somewhere really fun? Write it down! Did you make a new friend on your trip? Use the space at the end to write down their name and information to keep in touch!

There are **7 days' worth of pages**. Each day provides multiple pages for you to write all about your experiences and adventures at the many parks and attractions. Write about what you did, where you went and what you liked about it!

A NOTE TO PARENTS...

Encourage your child to take notes and write their experiences in this journal. Help them if they have any questions and be supportive of their work. Creativity is a great thing and by remembering the trip through their own experiences and feelings, they will create a memory that will truly last a lifetime.

Take a moment each day to sit down with your child and discuss how the day went in their eyes and help them to write down their thoughts. One day you will all look back on this journal and laugh and smile at the memories that were made.

Tips for getting ready for your trip.

1) Get Ready! Think about what you will need to do before leaving. Do you need someone to watch your dog? Is there anything that needs returned to the library or school? Make a list and check them off when you complete them.

2) What do I need to take along? Think about what kinds of toys, clothes or games you want to take with you. Remember that smaller items are easier to pack. So plan ahead!

3) Learn about where you are going. Use the Internet (or books) to learn more about the places you plan to visit while at Disney. Make a list of interesting things and what you want to see or do. Share what you learned with your group to help them learn too!

4) Have fun! Any trip away from home can be a great adventure and a lot of fun. Be willing to try new things and do something someone else wants to do, even if it doesn't sound fun to you. You never know, you might like it!

5) Entertain yourself
Take along this journal as well as some other activities to keep you busy along the way. We recommend the book "*Are We There Yet?*" which has tons of fun games to keep your whole family entertained while traveling.

Preparing for my trip to Disney!

Where am I staying?

_____

(What's the name of your hotel or resort? Are you staying at a friend or relative's house?)

How am I getting there?

_____

(Are you going by car, airplane, or train?)

How far away is it?

_____

(How many miles is it from your home to your destination?)

Who is going?

_____

(Is your brother going along? What about mom, dad, grandma, or a friend?)

What I need to do before I leave:

(See page 3 for tips on what to put here. Check the box when you have
completed or taken care of that item.)

☐ _____

☐ _____

☐ _____

☐ _____

☐ _____

☐ _____

☐ _____

☐ _____

☐ _____

☐ _____

☐ _____

☐ _____

☐ _____

☐ _____

Things I want to take with me:
(See page 3 for tips on what to put here. Check the box beside each item after it is packed. Don't forget your toothbrush and sunscreen!)

- [ ] _____
- [ ] _____
- [ ] _____
- [ ] _____
- [ ] _____
- [ ] _____
- [ ] _____
- [ ] _____
- [ ] _____
- [ ] _____
- [ ] _____
- [ ] _____
- [ ] _____
- [ ] _____

What do I want to see and do on my trip?

(See page 3 for tips on what to put here.)

1) _____

2) _____

3) _____

4) _____

5) _____

6) _____

7) _____

8) _____

9) _____

10) _____

11) _____

12) _____

Who to send postcards to:

(Show them you care by sending a note!)

Post Card

Place Stamp Here

Name: _____

Address: _____

City: _____ State _____ Zip _____

Name: _____

Address: _____

City: _____ State _____ Zip _____

Name: _____

Address: _____

City: _____ State _____ Zip _____

Name: _____

Address: _____

City: _____ State _____ Zip _____

Expectations:

Use this area to write about what you think will happen on your trip. For example, do you expect to see Mickey Mouse, Pluto or some other character? Do you think you'll ride a certain ride or go to a fun restaurant? Try to predict the future and see how things turn out!

Do this part BEFORE leaving!

_____

_____

_____

_____

_____

Fun facts about where I'm going:

(Write a few interesting facts about where you are going.)

1) _____

2) _____

3) _____

4) _____

5) _____

6) _____

Disney vacation - Day 1

Today's date: _____

Today's weather:

Today we visited:
(circle the park you went to)

Magic Kingdom

Epcot

Animal Kingdom

Hollywood Studios

_____

(Write where you went if it wasn't one
of the main Disney parks.)

What I like best about today's park:

_____

_____

_____

_____

_____

Rides I rode today:

I thought it was (circle one):

☺ =Boring   ☺☺ = OK   ☺☺☺ = Fun

_____

_____

_____

_____

_____

_____

_____

_____

_____

_____

My favorite ride from today was:

_____

_____

because _____

_____

_____

Characters I got to see today:

_____   _____

_____   _____

_____   _____

_____   _____

_____   _____

A drawing about my day:

Other fun activities I did today:

(Did you ride the monorail? See a show? Eat somewhere fun?
Go swimming? Try something new?)

_____

_____

_____

_____

_____

_____

Something I want to remember from

today is: _____

_____

_____

_____

Disney vacation - Day 2

Today's date: _____

Today's weather:

Today we visited:
(circle the park you went to)

Magic Kingdom

Epcot

Animal Kingdom

Hollywood Studios

_____

(Write where you went if it wasn't one
of the main Disney parks.)

What I like best about today's park:

_____

_____

_____

_____

_____

Rides I rode today:

_____

_____

_____

_____

_____

_____

_____

_____

_____

_____

_____

I thought it was (circle one):

☺ =Boring   ☺☺ = OK   ☺☺☺ = Fun

My favorite ride from today was:

_____

_____

because _____

_____

_____

Characters I got to see today:

_____   _____

_____   _____

_____   _____

_____   _____

_____   _____

A drawing about my day:

Other fun activities I did today:

(Did you ride the monorail? See a show? Eat somewhere fun?
Go swimming? Try something new?)

_____

_____

_____

_____

_____

_____

Something I want to remember from

today is: _____

_____

_____

_____

_____

Disney vacation - Day 3

Today's date: _____

Today's weather:

Today we visited:

(circle the park you went to)

Magic Kingdom

Epcot

Animal Kingdom

Hollywood Studios

_____

(Write where you went if it wasn't one of the main Disney parks.)

What I like best about today's park:

_____

_____

_____

_____

_____

Rides I rode today:

I thought it was (circle one):

$\smile$ = Boring　　$\smile\smile$ = OK　　$\smile\smile\smile$ = Fun

_____

_____

_____

_____

_____

_____

_____

_____

_____

_____

_____

My favorite ride from today was:

_____

_____

because _____

_____

_____

Characters I got to see today:

_____   _____

_____   _____

_____   _____

_____   _____

_____   _____

A drawing about my day:

Other fun activities I did today:

(Did you ride the monorail? See a show? Eat somewhere fun?
Go swimming? Try something new?)

_____

_____

_____

_____

_____

_____

Something I want to remember from

today is: _____

_____

_____

_____

_____

Disney vacation - Day 4

Today's date: _____

Today's weather:

Today we visited:

(circle the park you went to)

Magic Kingdom

Epcot

Animal Kingdom

Hollywood Studios

_____

(Write where you went if it wasn't one of the main Disney parks.)

What I like best about today's park:

_____

_____

_____

_____

_____

Rides I rode today:

I thought it was (circle one):

=Boring   = OK   = Fun

_____

_____

_____

_____

_____

_____

_____

_____

_____

_____

_____

My favorite ride from today was:

_____

_____

because _____

_____

_____

Characters I got to see today:

_____   _____

_____   _____

_____   _____

_____   _____

_____   _____

A drawing about my day:

Other fun activities I did today:

(Did you ride the monorail? See a show? Eat somewhere fun?
Go swimming? Try something new?)

_____

_____

_____

_____

_____

_____

Something I want to remember from

today is: _____

_____

_____

_____

_____

Disney vacation - Day 5

Today's date: _____

Today's weather:

Magic Kingdom

Epcot

Animal Kingdom

Hollywood Studios

Today we visited:
(circle the park you went to)

_____

(Write where you went if it wasn't one of the main Disney parks.)

What I like best about today's park:

_____

_____

_____

_____

_____

Rides I rode today:

_____

_____

_____

_____

_____

_____

_____

_____

_____

_____

I thought it was (circle one):

= Boring   = OK   = Fun

My favorite ride from today was:

_____

_____

because _____

_____

_____

Characters I got to see today:

_____   _____

_____   _____

_____   _____

_____   _____

_____   _____

A drawing about my day:

Other fun activities I did today:

(Did you ride the monorail? See a show? Eat somewhere fun?
Go swimming? Try something new?)

_____

_____

_____

_____

_____

_____

Something I want to remember from

today is: _____

_____

_____

_____

_____

Disney vacation - Day 6

Today's date: _____

Today's weather:

Today we visited:
(circle the park you went to)

Magic Kingdom

Epcot

Animal Kingdom

Hollywood Studios

_____

(Write where you went if it wasn't one
of the main Disney parks.)

What I like best about today's park:

_____

_____

_____

_____

_____

Rides I rode today:

_____	
_____	
_____	
_____	
_____	
_____	
_____	
_____	
_____	
_____	
_____	

I thought it was (circle one):

= Boring   = OK   = Fun

My favorite ride from today was:

_____

_____

because _____

_____

_____

Characters I got to see today:

_____   _____

_____   _____

_____   _____

_____   _____

_____   _____

A drawing about my day:

Other fun activities I did today:

(Did you ride the monorail? See a show? Eat somewhere fun?
Go swimming? Try something new?)

○ _____

○ _____

○ _____

○ _____

○ _____

○ _____

Something I want to remember from

today is: _____

_____

_____

_____

_____

Disney vacation - Day 7

Today's date: _____

Today's weather:

Today we visited:
(circle the park you went to)

Magic Kingdom

Epcot

Animal Kingdom

Hollywood Studios

_____
(Write where you went if it wasn't one
of the main Disney parks.)

What I like best about today's park:

_____

_____

_____

_____

_____

Rides I rode today:

_____

_____

_____

_____

_____

_____

_____

_____

_____

_____

I thought it was (circle one):

= Boring   = OK   = Fun

My favorite ride from today was:

_____

_____

because _____

_____

_____

Characters I got to see today:

_____   _____

_____   _____

_____   _____

_____   _____

_____   _____

A drawing about my day:

Other fun activities I did today:

(Did you ride the monorail? See a show? Eat somewhere fun?
Go swimming? Try something new?)

_____

_____

_____

_____

_____

_____

Something I want to remember from

today is: _____

_____

_____

_____

_____

My new friends!

(People I met while on my trip.)

Name: _____

Address: _____

City: _____ State _____ Zip _____

Email Address: _____

Phone Number: _____

Name: _____

Address: _____

City: _____ State _____ Zip _____

Email Address: _____

Phone Number: _____

Name: _____

Address: _____

City: _____ State _____ Zip _____

Email Address: _____

Phone Number: _____

Things I bought to remember this trip:

Item: Price

_____ $ _____

_____ $ _____

_____ $ _____

_____ $ _____

_____ $ _____

_____ $ _____

Memories I don't want to forget:

Use this area to write anything about your trip that you didn't write down already. Did your trip go the way you expected it to? Re-read your expectations and compare.

_____

_____

_____

_____

_____

_____

_____

_____

Other memories I want to remember!

(Tape or glue tickets, photos, postcards, maps, and other items here to remember your trip! Or write more about your adventures. It's up to you!)

Other memories I want to remember!

(Tape or glue tickets, photos, postcards, maps, and other items here to remember your trip! Or write more about your adventures. It's up to you!)

Other memories I want to remember!

(Tape or glue tickets, photos, postcards, maps, and other items here to remember your trip! Or write more about your adventures. It's up to you!)

Other memories I want to remember!

(Tape or glue tickets, photos, postcards, maps, and other items here to remember your trip! Or write more about your adventures. It's up to you!)

Other memories I want to remember!

(Tape or glue tickets, photos, postcards, maps, and other items here to remember your trip! Or write more about your adventures. It's up to you!)

Epcot World Showcase Passport

If you visit Epcot, be sure to get your passport stamped at each country!

To get stamped, you will need to visit the Kidcot station located within each country and ask a cast member to stamp your passport. Some Kidcot stations are easy to find, while others are a bit more hidden making your adventure around the world even more exciting. If you have trouble, just ask a cast member and look for the sign.

At each station you will be able to get your passport stamped and even have a cast member write a special note — usually in their native language!

Mexico

(stamp)

Norway

(stamp)

_____

_____

_____

_____

_____

_____

_____

China

(stamp)

_____

_____

_____

_____

_____

_____

_____

Germany

(stamp)

_____

_____

_____

_____

_____

_____

_____

Italy

(stamp)

United States

(stamp)

Japan

(stamp)

_____

_____

_____

_____

_____

_____

_____

Morocco

(stamp)

_____

_____

_____

_____

_____

_____

_____

France

(stamp)

_____

_____

_____

_____

_____

_____

_____

United Kingdom

(stamp)

_____

_____

_____

_____

_____

_____

_____

Canada

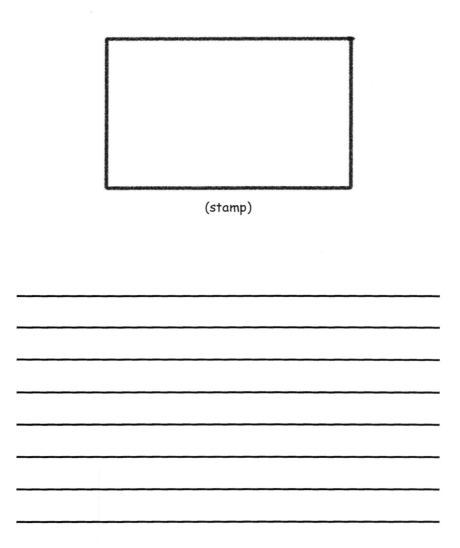

(stamp)

Disney World Scavenger Hunts

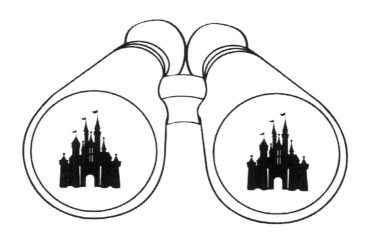

When you visit the Walt Disney World Resort parks, there are a lot of things to see and do. Why not make your visit even more fun by trying to find all of the items listed on the following pages for each park. These items can be found throughout the park and are in no particular order, so always be on the look out!

When you find one of the items, cross it off. See if you can find them all!

Good luck!

Magic Kingdom

- ☺ Monorail
- ☺ Someone wearing Mouse ears
- ☺ Statue of Walt Disney
- ☺ A train
- ☺ A map
- ☺ A balloon
- ☺ A horse
- ☺ A castle
- ☺ A popcorn cart
- ☺ A big tree house
- ☺ A flying elephant
- ☺ A pirate
- ☺ A spaceship
- ☺ A princess
- ☺ A former President of the U.S.A
- ☺ A tea cup
- ☺ A flying carpet
- ☺ Winnie the Pooh
- ☺ Mickey Mouse

Epcot

- ☺ Giant silver sphere
- ☺ Monorail
- ☺ Characters made out of plants
- ☺ A planet
- ☺ Someone wearing a sombrero
- ☺ Statue of a viking
- ☺ A Chinese building
- ☺ Statue of a horse
- ☺ American Flag
- ☺ A clock tower
- ☺ A park bench
- ☺ A double-decker bus
- ☺ A street band
- ☺ A "Kidcot" sign
- ☺ Coral Reef
- ☺ Nemo
- ☺ Sea Turtle
- ☺ Any live Disney character
- ☺ A dinosaur

Animal Kingdom

- ☺ Tree of Life
- ☺ Statue of a Disney character
- ☺ A dinosaur
- ☺ Live elephant
- ☺ A large mountain
- ☺ Live gorilla
- ☺ A train
- ☺ A safari vehicle
- ☺ Flik (the ant from "A Bug's Life)
- ☺ A stream / water flowing
- ☺ A balloon
- ☺ Someone wearing a safari hat
- ☺ Someone wearing a vest
- ☺ Any live Disney character
- ☺ A bus
- ☺ Dinosaur bones
- ☺ Truck selling Ice Cream
- ☺ Street band
- ☺ Rafiki (baboon from "The Lion King")

Hollywood Studios

- ☺ Magician's hat
- ☺ 1950's diner
- ☺ Giant Guitar
- ☺ Kermit the Frog
- ☺ Star Wars character
- ☺ Tower of Terror
- ☺ Giant letter blocks
- ☺ Woody or Jessie
- ☺ Beauty or the Beast
- ☺ Cinderella's Carriage
- ☺ Large green army men
- ☺ A giant ant or bug
- ☺ Mater
- ☺ Pizza Planet
- ☺ The Little Mermaid
- ☺ Mickey Mouse balloon
- ☺ Handprints in cement on walkways
- ☺ Mouse ears on a water tower
- ☺ A Spaceship

Character Autographs

Take the magic of Disney home with you by getting the autograph of all your favorite Disney characters. Mickey, Minnie, Cinderella, Belle, Ariel and all your new friends can write special messages on their own page during your visit, giving you a lasting memory of your adventures and experiences.

With 40 pages of autograph pages, there is enough room for all of your favorites!

Character Autographs

Character Autographs

Character Autographs

Character Autographs

Character Autographs

Character Autographs

Character Autographs

Character Autographs

Character Autographs

Character Autographs

Character Autographs

Character Autographs

Character Autographs

Character Autographs

Character Autographs

Character Autographs

Character Autographs

Character Autographs

Character Autographs

Character Autographs

Character Autographs

Character Autographs

Character Autographs

Character Autographs

Character Autographs

Character Autographs

Character Autographs

Character Autographs

Character Autographs

Character Autographs

Character Autographs

Character Autographs

Character Autographs

Character Autographs

Character Autographs

Character Autographs

Character Autographs

Character Autographs

Character Autographs

Character Autographs

Character Autographs

Games and Activities

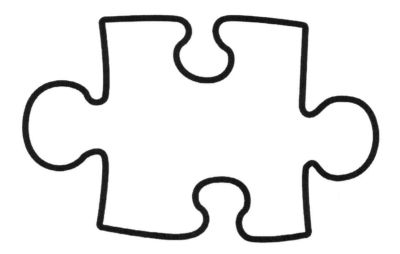

We all know that Walt Disney World has a ton of fun attractions and rides for you to enjoy. But there may be times when you want to just sit down and relax or are patiently waiting for your turn to ride.

Here are a few games you can play while waiting in line for a ride or hanging out at your hotel room.

Enjoy!

Hidden Mickeys

This game can be played anywhere at Disney (ride queues, restaurants, hotels, sidewalks, stores, horses). This fun-filled game will have you searching high and low for Mickey Mouse heads. Keep your eyes peeled for the character's signature head and ears combination. You'll be surprised where you find him!

Hidden Mickeys are everywhere, and though they are sometimes hard to find, a hidden Mickey should not have to rely too much on imagination. If you must squint your eyes, tilt your head, or have a certain amount of lighting at a certain angle, it's probably not a Mickey. It might just be a coincidental design. A Mickey may be upside down or sideways, but when pointed out, should be relatively clear and unique to its surroundings.

There are thousands of hidden mickeys scattered throughout the Walt Disney World Resort, so you will never run out of places to look!

I Spy

One person starts by finding something around them — it must be in clear view and visible by everyone. They then describe the item by giving everyone else clues. Whoever guesses what the item is first gets to find the next item.

Odds or Evens

Two players pick either "odds" or "evens." They then make a fist, shake it, say "one, two, three, shoot" and stick out either one or two fingers. If the total is an odd number then "odds" wins. If it is an even number, "evens" wins.

Don't Say "Um"

Pick a topic and go around your group and see if each person can talk about the topic for 20 seconds without using the words "um," "hmm," "let's see," or without making any long pauses. It is harder than it sounds!

How many words can you make using letters in:

Walt Disney World

_____ _____ _____

_____ _____ _____

_____ _____ _____

_____ _____ _____

_____ _____ _____

_____ _____ _____

_____ _____ _____

_____ _____ _____

_____ _____ _____

_____ _____ _____

_____ _____ _____

_____ _____ _____

_____ _____ _____

_____ _____ _____

_____ _____ _____

_____ _____ _____

_____ _____ _____

How many words can you make using letters in:

Animal Kingdom

_____	_____	_____
_____	_____	_____
_____	_____	_____
_____	_____	_____
_____	_____	_____
_____	_____	_____
_____	_____	_____
_____	_____	_____
_____	_____	_____
_____	_____	_____
_____	_____	_____
_____	_____	_____
_____	_____	_____
_____	_____	_____
_____	_____	_____
_____	_____	_____

How many words can you make using letters in:

Hollywood Studios

_____   _____   _____

_____   _____   _____

_____   _____   _____

_____   _____   _____

_____   _____   _____

_____   _____   _____

_____   _____   _____

_____   _____   _____

_____   _____   _____

_____   _____   _____

_____   _____   _____

_____   _____   _____

_____   _____   _____

_____   _____   _____

_____   _____   _____

_____   _____   _____

_____   _____   _____

Made in the USA
Columbia, SC
30 December 2018